The Share

JANE MONSON

Published by Cinnamon Press
Meirion House,
Glan yr afon,
Tanygrisiau
Blaenau Ffestiniog,
Gwynedd, LL41 3SU
www.cinnamonpress.com
The right of Jane Monson to be identified as author of this work has been asserted by her in accordance with the Copyright, Designs and Patent Act, 1988. Copyright © 2013 Jane Monson
ISBN: 978-1-907090-95-0

British Library Cataloguing in Publication Data. A CIP record for this book can be obtained from the British Library.

All rights reserved. No part of this publication may be reproduced, stored in a retrieval system, or transmitted in any form or by any means, electronic, mechanical, photocopying, recording or otherwise without the prior written permission of the publishers. This book may not be lent, hired out, resold or otherwise disposed of by way of trade in any form of binding or cover other than that in which it is published, without the prior consent of the publishers.

Designed and typeset in Palatino by Cinnamon Press
Cover from original artwork 'dilapidated room' by Ryan 0179 © Ryan 0179, agency: dreamstime.com
Cover design by Jan Fortune

Printed in Poland

Cinnamon Press is represented in the UK by Inpress Ltd www.inpressbooks.co.uk and in Wales by the Welsh Books Council www.cllc.org.uk

Acknowledgments

'Derwent the Boy, Derwent the River' uses the following lines from Coleridge's Notebooks:
'that for the first time in his consciousness, he became giddy...turned pale with fright and repeatedly cried – 'The Kissen is walking away from Derwent'
'and finding that he could not speak, he turned pale as death and in the reaction from fear flushed red and gave [him] a blow in the face.'
Coleridge's Notebooks: A Selection edited by Perry (OUP, 2002) p.29, used by kind permission of Oxford University Press.

'Beam of Light' won 2nd prize in the Café Writers Competition 2012 – thanks to Ian Duhig and the Committee.

'Crossing the Salt' appeared in the Special Sheffield Poetry Festival edition of *Antiphon,* issue 7, Spring 2013. Thanks to all involved, especially, River Wolton and Donna Stonecipher for the brilliant and memorable Prose Poetry Festival and reading.

Warm appreciation to Table 20 and Chloe Szebrat for her time and encouragement. Thanks to the very appreciated Andy Brown for his time and useful comments, all taken in. To Ben Walker for his enthusiastic read-through and inspired list of books and all at CUP Bookshop for their generous support and interest. A warm thank you to CB1 Poetry for the airing some of the poems have received. To the brilliant writing group in Muswell Hill and in memory of Jean and Maria – what they gave and still give. To Gordon, my family and friends, here and abroad. Love, thanks and appreciation to the Sotudeh family, and to Niki, in particular, for his loving support, sharp eyes and ears and ways of being there.

Finally, to Jan, Rowan and Cottia for their positive dedication to Cinnamon Press and all their authors.

Contents

The Photograph	9
Table Manners	10
A Wolf at My Table	11
The Un-Table	12
No Shooting at the Table	13
The Tuscan Table	14
The Hermit's Table	15
The Grey Area	16
Turning the Tables	17
Journey towards Dinner	18
Still Life	19
In Difference	20
Tongue Twister	21
No Listening at the Table	22
The Naked Table	23
The Cool Hands of Luke	24
Bone China	25
Frank Sinatra attempts to yank table-cloth, Miami, 1964-65	26
Table of Forgetting	27
Dressed-up, Washed-up	28
Table Service	29
The Order of Things	30
Sailing at Tables	31
Crossing the Salt	32
The Inherited Surface	33
Wife, Table, Cake	34
The Absence	35
'Mirror on Way'	36
The White Ribbon	37
The Lowering of Heads	38
Play in the Rehearsal	39
Apple for Teeth	40
Table Memoir	41
After Buñuel: *The Phantom of Liberty*	42
The Gap in the Resolute Desk	43
Derwent the Boy, Derwent the River	44
Beam of Light	45
Of Kings and Men	46

Invisible People	47
The Author's Tour	48
The Book Launch	49
At R. S. Thomas's Table	50
The Wait	51
The Shared Surface	52
The Chipping Forecast	53
Square of Light: The Artist is Present I	54
The Artist is Present II	55
About the Author	57

To Niki and our forthcoming

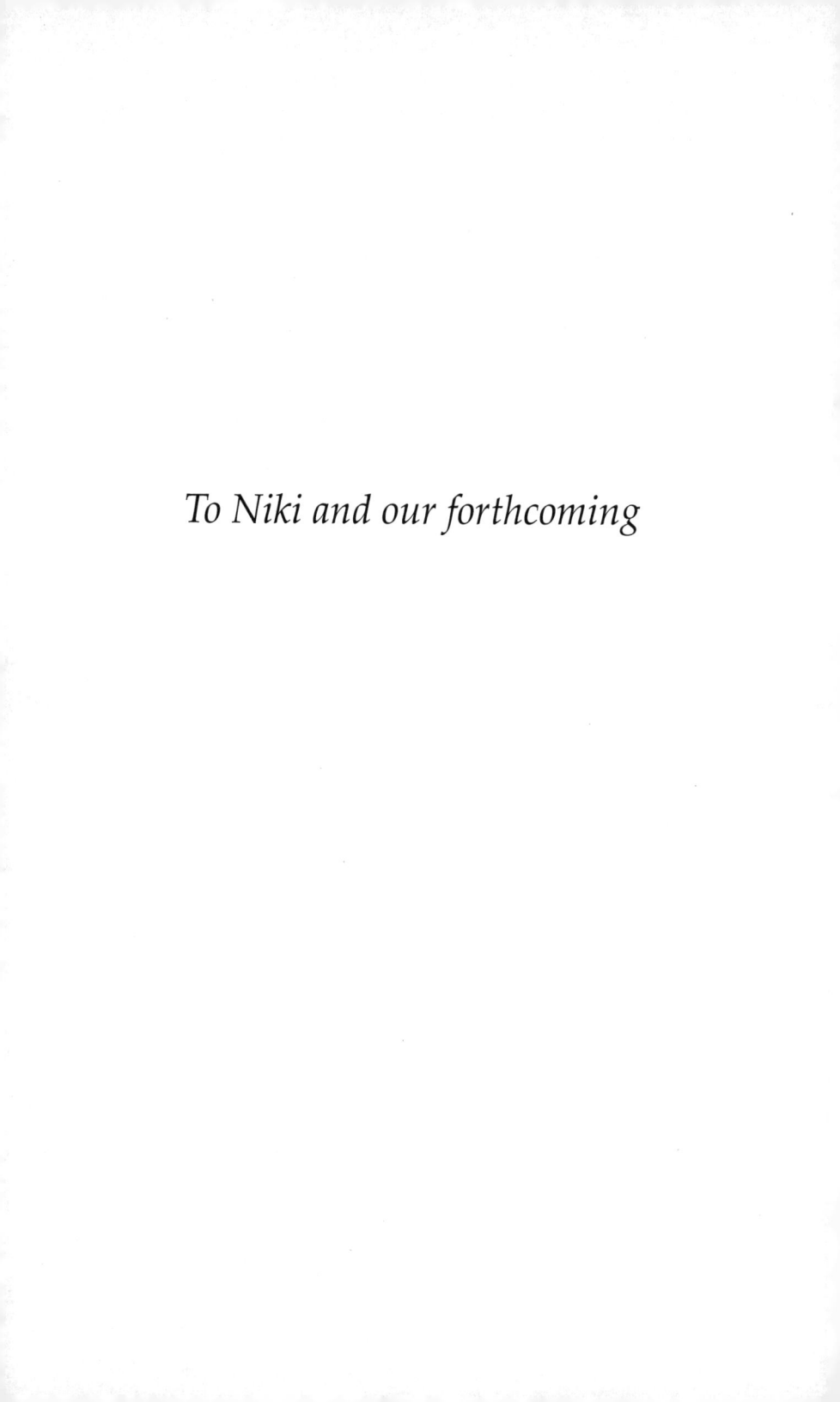

The Shared Surface

The Photograph

Only parts of her face are lit, but she knows that's her mother. She is at the far end of the table, where the shadows collect; her gaze is comforted there. She would rather sink into the dark than into the lined face of her father. He is turning away from his wife; she is part of his skin's tale. He only looks at her when he needs something, or when she shouts 'no!' Otherwise he follows his knife and fork, the food disappearing in measured, carefully timed bites. Nobody speaks of anything. The table keeps quiet. She wonders if her mother's mouth is open to attempt food or speech. She tries to hear her thoughts in the black and white, but only gets the puncture of steel in potatoes, the scrape of metal herding peas and the clink of a ring as a glass is levered up and down with frequency. 'Every time I turn on a light in this house I get an electric shock!' her grandmother shouts and walks out the door before the meal is over. And so the rest of us are left, still not speaking, but wondering: who is trying to kill who and is that our cue to speak, or be excused?

Table Manners

They have made a promise not to argue this evening, but to pass a pleasant war-free dinner. Blood is shed before they sit down. The hostess has asked that men and women alternate each other, so that the table reads, man, woman, man, woman, man, woman etc. By the time she spells this out, one side of the table is ruffled male, the other tutting female. Halfway through the starter course – a single bed of lettuce – the man with the beard who has trouble with silence, declares with thrust-out fork, that this is the finest lettuce he's ever chewed. Calmly, the hostess thanks him and asks him to sit down. The dandelion wine that was going to be avoided is opened and splashed into all the tumblers. It is a drink with a brief delayed reaction and after the first sip with a smile, each guest chokes, spits, coughs red, or hiccups. Afterwards, one man stabs in the dark with the weather. It's been almost worth mentioning, but after the effortful hum of appreciation, his wife grows tense and the others sniff it out like dogs. 'I could be at home, working,' she begins. They all have somewhere they could be is the consensus, but they are here, sitting on their hands and bottling their throats with soup and lettuce. The hostess takes their lids off, blows their game completely and arrows the truth home. They all look shot, pin-cushioned at first, then almost drowned, gasping for air and a passing rock. When all hell breaks free, the table asks to be excused.

A Wolf at My Table

The children bring live crabs in yellow buckets to the breakfast table. They leak a portion of sea over the tapestried carpet and the sound of sand grinds loudly in their father's ear. He explodes porridge and china into their faces: My God! Animals! Not children, animals! It is the mother's fault. She has unlearnt the manners he's set for them all. While she knits, darns so their socks go round and round their age, the stitching of the house comes undone. But, she could retort, while he writes and appears only when food is on the table, the talk dies, the stuff that makes them withers. The children quickly follow their rivers out; run back to the sea to empty their buckets. When they return, their father has fastened himself up to the neck, but the red is slowly fading from his skin. He looks out across the painted china, the engraved silver and finely cut glass, and in his soldiered voice, tells them when to pass this and when to pass that, and eyelet by eyelet, to undo their little mouths and tell him what they have planned for today, what they have learnt from yesterday, and how it will improve their tomorrow. They are past stuttering these days, feed him titbits. The day he returned their waking shells to the sea, undid their work, they made a pact: to cut him loose and follow in her weave; unlearn yesterday with each row, each dropped stitch, each song, down to every sharp note.

The Un-Table

A cartoon of a parent holds a paper whose front headline reads: 'Families struggle to put food on table.' The young tubby son takes in the statement, and over-replete with chips, asks: 'What's a table?' Where does the parent begin? A table is a place we've never been and never need to go. A table is our missing host to food. We carry things for it instead. A table is the street; in transit, between take-away and home. A table takes up space we can use for other things; our outstretched legs, a cushion, a cat. A table is a risk. An open field for all sorts of possibilities, including fights, spillage, breakage, silence. When I was your age we had a table. We knew all these possibilities, the limits between the edges, the cost of elbows on wood, talking across our elders. On or underneath or around the thing, we never knew how to behave. Best not to complicate the room, but leave it as it is.

No Shooting at the Table

When he was a boy, he ran around the table with a gun. Not a toy gun, but a real one, normally stored in a cupboard for hunting. No pretend sounds of Bang! Bang! just a boy silently encircling his family while holding the thing and rushing its nose behind their petrified heads.

When he was a man, a car he was in wobbled to a halt, somewhere in the country; juddered into silence by a field-lined road. No jack to hand, he lifted the Citroën while his brother slid underneath to change the wheel. 'I'll let go now shall I?' Out shot his brother from under the metal grave. 'I was only joking,' he said. 'Well you wouldn't have been in the old days,' his brother fired back.

No harm ever came to any of them. Whatever it was in him, puzzled him the most. The jokes as he saw them, with gun or car in hand, were only ever recounted at tables. While we would go round and round hunting the answers, he only ever settled on the questions, always with tea in one hand, pipe in the other, pointing out the places where the smoke and the steam collided.

The Tuscan Table

Just before they'd had a chance to serve, something forced their exit. A war perhaps? Though the stillness in the wooden plates, the cups and rested table-dust infer that destruction had no place here. A message then? Someone they had to run towards, someone they couldn't leave once they were there? Droppings from mice and birds mixed in with the dust and debris cover suggestions, clues. There are no chair scrapes in the floorboards, though the seats approach the table in different ways, their expressions dignified, or spellbound. One looks towards the door, like an expectant child, a pair almost face each other in timeless conference, and one is pushed into the table, as though scolded, but determined to face the consequences. No trace of hand nor feet anymore, the prompted exeunt is an old tale; the story of a thousand Tuscan houses, silent shells for tables, dined then undined. They call the villages of the houses, ghost villages, *paesi fantasma*. Articles blame landslides, migrations, poverty. The trained eyes and shoes of intermittent strangers scan the floors and walls and ceilings; trace the light fittings and furniture in important voices, take notes, images, but the things refuse to divulge the truth. The chairs, the table won't betray the room, they have no interest in our interest; get stored in lists for a while, archived in pictures and for centuries reflect back what we don't know. In the houses of the living, the houses of the dead are discussed; their empty plates, our groaning tables, their perpetual night, our chase by day.

The Hermit's Table

It looks like hiding, not living, the cave in the rock face with a beige door and black window. We stare from hundreds of feet below, eyes straining through cameras and heat waves, willing the door to open, to be ushered in and asked to sit at the Hermit's table. But door and table alike are unwilling; kept as the very least of our thresholds. This is where the passing through and placing of ourselves ends. Here is where we reflect on the cloths we have bent over in churches, hosting symbols and prayers; on deserted villages where we fell out of line and found our own surface. Tired, burnt, covered in dust, we drank and washed at springs, breathed in heavy, but satisfied sighs, ate at crumbled walls, at tables of rotting and devoured wood, wrestled with cameras, pointed and followed the rare goat. Our meeting points became celebrations; we revived our spirits in ghost-towns, and though cold and unlit, the houses helped us to feel human again, just as the churches stopped us moving and changed our direction. But the house in the Gorge's face tells us who we are and are not, puts us in our place, as passers-by, as curious, as outsiders, baking to death, blind, hungry with anticipation.

The Grey Area

When she's dark, Jesus faces the wall; when she's light, she goes out to the garden. But since he's left, she's undecided, sloshing about the grey area, pacing, waiting, while her hands fidget somewhere between roses and religion. She feels it most at the table. To set or not to set, to sit or not to sit. In the mist she reasons that something has to break and appear. Less a blinding light, than a solid shape on the horizon demanding a decision or a fine-tuned thought. Her mother wouldn't suffer this. Her father might. Her grandmother certainly wouldn't. When her husband left, she poisoned the Willow tree he'd planted and axed it to the height of a low stool. At this thought, her hands stop moving without purpose, take her over to the wall, unhook his Grace and put him in the attic. Outside, summer isn't over and there is plenty of garden to bring into the house. Filling a crystal vase, she places ten cut stems with red velvet heads in the centre of the table, goes back, plucks fresh green pods from their stakes and plans a meal around rolling hot buttered peas. Table talk tonight would revolve around unseen shifts, her glass would toast decisively. The faces of flowers would open according to different shades of candlelight, green eyes would glisten under the butter's melt, and her old lover's collection would spin songs in the corner, making webs for her to walk through on her way outside.

Turning the Tables

He lights six candles to get the tone of her skin to his taste. When she enters the room, he pulls out a chair, gestures with an open palm that she should sit here. She paces the table instead, stops at the candles and moves one finger through its flame, darkening her skin and releasing a puff of smoke into the atmosphere. She chooses a place of her own, and the other guests appear through the door, their gowns flooding and fussing round the chairs. The seat next to hers stays empty and he moves into it gratefully, settling himself in a manner slightly above his age. When the first course arrives, pea and cider soup, he keeps half an eye on the dip of his spoon, remembering to journey it away from his face before bringing it back, and half an eye on her, consciously doing the same. When the second course arrives – sea bass, potatoes, peas, one lemon slice per plate – he studies the fish knife, cross-eyed, for slightly too long and she kicks him gently under the table, her shoes laughing to the floor, mid the otherwise gentile flock of feet. By the time they have finished the torte, their ankles and calves are very well acquainted. When coffee is brought in, she moves forward, into the table, with discretion, commands her left arm to his right thigh, lifts his gown to a sudden cough and in lipstick writes her room number over his skin. 'Is something the matter?' one of the guest's remarks like a teacher about to ask him to stand up and read the note aloud. 'No, nothing, nothing,' he throws back, too fast, too high, prematurely concerned he'll get caught by a slight misapprehension of a woman's hand.

Journey towards Dinner

A man on a train reads his novel as he would hold the features of his wife. The book is taken up in his hands, her face raised to his eyes, the lines reflected in his glasses, his palms slightly curved around her cheeks. Taking in her mouth, the leaves close to his skin, he is lost in the print of her speaking. She smells sweet and dry, of sun-aged paper and type: honey, hazelnut and leather. He smoothes the pages flat along the spine; her skin under his fingers sounds like Autumn being moved around a far-flung road. His station is announced and the nightmare of grunting elbows, knees, jackets, briefcases, newspapers and phones clatters his head back into focus. He closes her face, gets up and is moved onto the platform by the crowd. The man goes home to where she might be or where the impression of her most definitely is. At dinner she'll ask him why he's late. I missed my stop, he'll lie. When they settle more into sitting opposite each other, she'll ask him for the truth and he'll tell her in the only way he can when put on the spot: he was thinking about her as his paperback; forgetting his book as an object and being overcome by her in his hands. She won't ask for the truth again.

Still Life

Aubergine folds in tongues from the blade's strike and is gathered on a plate of salt to yield. Oil bleeds across the pan, heats up into a spit where the flesh is laid, scorched and scarred. Transfigured, quiet, the pieces are lifted, blotted with kitchen-paper, sprinkled with torn mint, bashed garlic and the rain of lime.

She settles the poultry in earthenware – beds the meat amid the autumn of red onion, sweet potato and bell peppers – glistens the content with a pool of wine and details the dish with the float of tarragon.

They wait outside the stove, thoughts somewhere between the changing smells of heat that turn and drift and their hands, still glowing from preparation. Inside the kitchen, the hum after the arrangement of chairs, the pulled-out table, the cold from china and steel, the run of water and the filling of things, where the waves rise and crash inside the glass walls. The timer itches on, the door will go soon. She hears his stomach growl, threaten to begin before the meal is ready.

In Difference

His fist pounds the table and makes the plates jump above the cloth. Water hiccups to the top of the glasses. She holds her breath. All of this has its own inevitability. Their lives have changed, upended, and this morning she just laid the table as usual; tightened her hands around fruit, squeezed oranges into a jug, lined up toast in the rack and on the hob, coffee bubbling up to the rim of the pan, a pond alive with frogs. She wants to get away, cross any old sea, so he, they can feel warm again, alive, out of suburbia's picket fences stitching and dividing all the lawns; away from the rarity of hello; streets blasted of leaves and raised by Sunday sculpted hedges. I'm looking for a way in, not out, she insists. He has made a fine hair line crack in one cup and a side plate from the wedding set is in two pieces, egg spilt into the fabric. He doesn't believe in gluing things back together. This is not a symbolic statement – he just believes in replacing. Based on this alone, their marriage has never been whole, fixable.

Tongue Twister

As they speak, the straw develops a split in its bendy neck. Binding her finger, she tells him about the conversation they had the other morning. That part of her hand can't breathe, he thinks. He watches the finger's fate and loses part of her sentence in the process. Responding to what he has heard she unwinds the plastic from her finger and looks at how her skin has become ridged and pale. The straw has gone from body to sack, sighing its last as she pushes it into the table and leaves. It reminds him of two things: a snake's shed skin and a snail's shed shell. He says these things to himself more than once, trying to repeat them quickly and perfectly before she returns.

No Listening at the Table

They have gone, the familiar faces round the table and in their place objects appear. An eye for bread, a tooth for a glass and a meal for the rest of the body. The salt won't pass itself, though alone, she asks it to anyway. There is no reason for seconds, but she asks politely anyway. Footsies with her mother rarely occurred, but she kicks up her shoe in her general direction, looks down at her plate intently, turns red and mumbles. She hears her brother giggle. Definitely hears her brother giggle. And was that her father's key turning? No, that was next door's father. She thinks of other uses for the chairs, contemplates inviting the toys downstairs, but sod's law, someone would pay her a visit. 'The lasagne is one of your best' she goes for and the room is filled with its rich homely scent and appreciation from all the family. The candles start to dribble onto the table and she sees herself wobble in the window. Picking up the bottle, she helps herself. The wine enlivens her own company and she leans over to the radio behind her plate, turns up the voices and settles back into whatever they have to say.

The Naked Table

Too early for dressing, the nude mahogany table settles for dust and the coming and going of sunlight, the quick land and launch of a fly, the passing gesture of a cup. At the opening and closing of doors, a dog pads in and in the absence of its master, gets up on its hind legs and punctuates the wood with yet another scratch and sniff. In between meals, the hands of the child slide whatever they have picked up that afternoon along the engraved edges, a trail of his adventures planted firmly inside its grain. When the sun drops behind the hills, a finger clicks on the overheads and the room reflects itself cinematically in windows. Under the spotlight's glare the wood is sprayed, polished, wiped of its thoughts and theirs, and muffled under the throw of a cloth. Pinned down at eight points by plates and glasses, then a further half a dozen as suitable garnishes adorn its otherwise scarred plane, the wood braces itself for another persecution: banged, heated, scalded, smeared and talked over. At its creak and shift as four pairs of elbows press its legs further into the floor, the table sighs, then groans audibly – no sooner has its body lightened as the food fills theirs, it has to suffer the inevitable after-dinner talk that this is their last meal at the dear old thing and they must remember tomorrow morning, to order the one with the wings and the honey-pine finish.

The Cool Hands of Luke

There is a table where taking away is giving. Where a prisoner is given too much food as punishment after his stomach has shrunk in a box, and spoon by spoon, fellow jailbirds, get up, walk over to his plate, and lift a mouthful of rice to their lips. He thinks of digging. Being made to dig his own grave the last four days before begging for mercy. And this is it. Mercy. A broken face over a lowering mound; the cycle of sun and road-weathered arms and cracked hands and tiny shovels coming in from behind him, taking away and giving. They are not just risking their souls, they are risking their spoons. From day one, the prisoners are commanded to hold onto their own; to share their steel with no one and if they fail, they go in the box. No tables in there of any kind. Just a floor and a pan and you with the thoughts you'd rather not be left alone with, digging out the dark and narrowing the air until they've had enough.

Bone China

In a fading room – by a pale, thin spread of evening light – appear a dozen old men and women. The occasional nod of understanding and shake of confusion lend the air brief shivers of time passing. Some hands pace the borders against the walls, others shuffle upright into their frames and the rest continually adjust to their seats.

Together they give the impression of gently billowing curtains, loosely tied and cloud-blown.

She watches their flesh chameleon with the light, then glimpses the possibility of change; catches it in the blush of excitement that travels bee-like, from face to face, as the door behind them opens then closes, fills the room with the scent of gravy and offers them the end of the day on a flock of white china plates.

Frank Sinatra attempts to yank table-cloth, Miami, 1964-65

The dates say it all. Between '64 and '65, Sinatra gathers the cloth into a tail and gets ready to pull the thing clean from under the dinner. Three shots: beginning, middle and end. Mouths agape, the crowd catches the sound of his cloaked laugh in their throats. In the first frame, the ketchup and glasses are standing, but at his accidental pull are already moving towards the edge, like children drawn in sleighs towards their first hill. One man puts a nail between his teeth, bites hard as he watches a portion of his restaurant in the amateur hand of the singer. In the second frame, his face is lit up under the roof of the cloth: it flies above their heads half-phantom, half sheet beneath which the children run and huddle before it swallows them whole. By the third frame, Sinatra holds the limp rag in his hand and open-mouthed looks off stage towards a shout. A woman flails backwards on her chair with delight. The head-waiter looks at the table: undressed, its objects in a heap in the middle, some tipped, but none broken, the exhausted napkins recovering over each other in petrified folds.

Table of Forgetting

New York, El Quijote restaurant, 1965. They seem to have been sitting there for days: Burroughs, Warhol, Smith, other artists and their patron, Grady, eating and talking in riddles and spoonerisms. At the head of the table, one arm across the patron's shoulders, Burroughs lifts a hand to pronounce what he's saying. At the table's foot, Warhol mirrors his eyes with dark glasses, looks directly at the camera, casts the man behind him in shadow. Opposite him two men hold their hands over their faces and the patron looks at them, their intelligent angel, amused and puzzled. The table looks shattered. Stained at the cloth, cigarettes hover their greying heads precariously over the linen and plates; bottles, glasses, cutlery are all askew, and napkins are at odds with each other, buckled, folded and hanging in various positions. They are the guests' broken wings, a flock of birds fallen dead at their elbows. Whatever has been said, is being said, can be read in the chaos of their arrangement, but at the announcement of a photograph, for a shuttered second, everything changes. The subject is thrown from the room by the man behind the camera and they are aware of nothing but themselves. Look closely and the faces behind the hands are peering through parted fingers, Burroughs' hand is not making a point, but trying to stop the aimed eye from shooting, and their patron is not looking amused, nor puzzled, but smiling at herself and her patronly ways. Under the words and the mess, the table continues her smile: new lines in the wood begin to form as more time goes by and the prospect of leaving its sides, less and less of an issue.

Dressed-up, Washed-up

They don't have very long to pass the salt. As they dine, the water begins to gather around their feet. The daughter insists on going out before the meal is over, but her outfit has caused offence and she is grounded. As the kitchen leak begins to flood the room, the boy's shoes are pulled by a wave from his feet and float off towards the living area. Still they eat and argue about the girl's dress. Wading in rubber boots between the counter and her family, the mother brings out seconds and says again, that it's not up for debate. The girl's lips are black, to match the shadows of her lids and her little brother only recognises her from certain angles. Directly opposite is not one of them. Racing the food into his stomach, the father is anxious about time. The rugby is about to begin and the television will need raising. The water reflects in silvery broken lines over the walls and ceiling and one by one the lamps are lifted onto the counters from the table and low surfaces. Nobody speaks when they sit down again, but stop up their mouths with their mother's best dish. The goldfish swims off towards the corridor. The cat scales recipe books up to the ceiling. The game is about to start. They swim the plates to the sink and ignore the wallowing glasses and cutlery. The girl forgets herself and joins the family in the living room where the television is above their heads, a sofa mounted onto a sofa where they climb and settle themselves before the light, the war-cry, the sun-dried skin, fixed eyes and wind-blown hair of the crowd. The family are quiet, absolutely still. The salt passed them a long, long time ago.

Table Service

The waiter rushes headless past their table, a black and white sketch of a thing, constantly becoming a memory or a man imagined. They look down to where the menu should be, re-settle their hollow gaze on a vase. Whoosh, there he goes again, west of their raised arms. The red flowers come under scrutiny; hunger begins to focus the couple. He pulls the glass towards him, splits the carnations, places some on her plate and eats his half with bare hands. She parts her jaw to speak, but is drowned out by the table next to them, howling at something the waiter said. Knife and fork in hand, she separates crowns and leaves from the stems as she would flesh from its bones, washes down her half with some of the water; he welcomes the rest and swills out petals from his teeth. They settle into the dining wood, the chequered cloth and pearly plates, raise their empty glasses and sharp knives to their faces, and watch each other through goldfish reflections and slivers of steel. An eye in the cutlery sees their hunger shift up a gear. One napkin, torn into scraps, past the lips and down the throat; 'mouth coils' of the magician's trick, but no ribbons stream from his face. Disappointed, she comfort eats; sucks table-cloth, napkins and cutlery inside her like spaghetti. He asks for the last word. Eats his own body-weight in plate, table and chairs. She rises, towers over him on the floor, swoops down and devours him whole, smacking her lips on the last thing he whispered, the last thing he saw, the last thing he heard, the last thing he almost did.

The Order of Things

The man who has been invited to dinner has ontological agnosia. If the napkins with the birds are put out, he will see sparrows flying about the table and do his best to get them outside. Windows will be opened, objects upset, and conversation embarrassed. The table must be made safe, agnosia-proof. Plain, image-less. All guests must be forewarned and told to wear blank clothes. At the last party, one man made the mistake of wearing a tie with clocks. They were all telling different times, and our man reached out to correct them all, but on being unable to find their dials, cursed, grappled at the man's chest and caused just enough discomfort. Later, at dessert, when the talk turned to absence, the man with the clock tie pulled out a photograph of his wife from his wallet. When he put her back, our man shouted him down, demanding he didn't stuff her in and suffocate the poor woman. No discussion ensued. Is there any safe ground we might ask? What about the paintings on the wall? One side, Turner's *London's Burning*, another Hopper's *Nighthawks*. He won't know where he is? How can an American forties diner occupy the same territory as the Houses of Parliament, on fire? So the room is stripped bare to avoid panic. The table is laid only with the things themselves, no patterns, nor pictures of things, just the reassuring solidity and actuality of the objects themselves, picked up, set down; at the mercy of us while the talk ticks boldly on.

Sailing at Tables

They sit opposite each other. The one who speaks first thinks they're on a ship and shouts *captain* and *starboard* across the table. The other who is getting the peas and fish keeps the ship sailing and does not break the story all evening. It is like sleep talking, he decides and it could get dangerous if he wakes his mouth and says what's really what. Prepare for docking, the chef declares, and anchors the plates down on the wood. Knife and fork get to work before the next wave and for a while the waters are calm, until the whisky insists all over his lap. 'We must have been hit,' says his passenger. He gets up, runs to the top of the stairs, up the ladder, through the attic, throws open the skylight to check the mast. The aerial nods it's OK. All the constellations are winking in code and the chef clambers up to the roof and translates The Big Dipper. 'We tapped the harbour walls landing and only the floor and trousers are damaged. Nobody has been hurt, but the fresh catch is losing flavour and the chairs are getting cold.' Downstairs, the room is indifferent when he makes another entrance, but he is quietly grateful the things are still standing, so takes his place at the head and begins to eat. Finally he finishes the food and ultimately the conversation. They're on a ship and he's shouting 'waving not drowning' across the table. The other tips the salt on purpose and flings far too much of it over his left shoulder.

Crossing the Salt

The thunder layers like ivy around the house and the lights and the film stop before the meal is over. A crack in the dark as the dog jaws a bone under the table, and the fast tick-tock of marbles gathering on the roof tiles as the sky falls lower, and the rain higher above the ground. Shutting the dog inside, its baying fading behind the door, we link arms, our faces shadowed under the umbrella and knock on doors to see how the villagers are handling the night, the one we made accidentally, spilling salt and crossing it with the wrong hand.

The Inherited Surface

Before she took a lover's whispers to heart, she set up a photograph of her mother on the table next to the bed and watched closely for his eyes to leave her. Garboesque bones, skin smooth as wax, hair rippled and glinting as the Mediterranean, Gaby would turn to the camera, her pouted mouth celebrating its gaze, crash after crash of light. Never in those moments of glory did she imagine to be dulled by dust on her daughter's bedside table and used to test her sex. 'Love me, loathe my mother' was Maria's way about love and if by the sepia still he read aloud Gaby's beauty, he would leave without a kiss goodnight, be asked to shut the door behind him, having barely warmed the bed, leaving mother and child alone in the black and white moonlight, each waiting for the other to smile.

Wife, Table, Cake

He reverses, backs the chair into a wall and something shoots from a perfect hole in his mouth. She inhales, taps ash into a jam jar, closes her eyes and curls her hand around the glass. 'I drawn forks about candle,' he proffers, dropping and sliding his finger over the table like a pen. She doesn't like correcting him anymore. Anymore than she likes guiding him back to bed in the middle of the night, from the road, the garden, the living room floor, the bath. Last night she found him in the kitchen, concentrated in the fridge-light, standing with his hands on the shelves moving the food about like Scrabble tiles, trying to spell his name in salad. He'd written for months by speaking and tracing the words over every surface in the house with his finger. Sometimes it became a race between his mouth and his hand, where he would hear himself say the word then chase his breath to the table, chair, wall, cupboards, oven and shelves, diving through the finish-line hand-first. She married him without a bomb in his brain; he would remain her husband until it went off. She recalled early signs of pressure, where sentences began to lose their stuffing; his face an open mouth at dinner or breakfast for long stretches like a sort of horrified yawn, where he meant to tell her about the day, but would pause and ask her to pass something instead – an elephant, the road, or her hair. Tonight, the same table, same wife, same glass, ash, wine, same man she's always known, just different words, different timing. And though she still recognises his voice and his hands, she watches them move against each other now, over all the surfaces and holes, just outside of her. Tonight, he misses her face by a whistle. Tonight, he blows on her skin and she pretends to go out.

The Absence

Sometimes he shaves himself, sometimes the mirror; the pillow of foam across his face, unscraped, left as old-fashioned snow, while the glass is marked rhythmically by a clean, but practised blade. Where he used to be by her side, she's now by her own; in supermarkets, in the car, all rooms of the house, at their meals, around the plates of others. Away from home, the surfaces and walls are all too confusing, the food on the plates too strange. She watches – in spite of herself – the knife and fork cut up the same piece of meat through the hour, the cold veg driven about the edges, the potato pushed to one side, then back again, prongs toying with the stuff like prey. What else is seen beyond the food, are the switches between concentration and loss. There it is, again and again, that exam-eye and brow, then a milky parting of ways, a failure of the mouth to grip thought and turn it outside. 'Where's Father Christmas?' he wants and doesn't want to know as he steps away from the resolute table legs. There is a warm murmur around their silence with all the words used to not answer this one way or the other. But somewhere on the inside, between all the nods and soft laughter is the place we don't know yet and fear: where you and your reflection don't separate anymore and the conversation at the table finally learns to stop.

'Mirror on Way'

Finishing, he zips, tightens his belt and walks over to the sink. Looking up at the framed glass, he finds nothing, a blank where his face should be. The water races through his hands, his heart hammers, full of false notes. He lowers himself over the basin, cups the stream and hurls it at his eyes. Raising his head again, he sees a sign next to the empty frame – a message in pencil with a child's arrow pointing across: 'Mirror on Way'. The white square grants him an outline, a dark cut-out of his shape. He wipes his hands on his jeans, brings them up to his face, looks at them, touches his skin and smoothes his hair; tames the silhouette, starts to settle into himself as a shadow. Back in the bar, he scans the queue of faces in the mirror behind the coloured bottles, picks hers out again. He wants to tell her about what just happened; about what didn't happen. How replacing the glass with paper has made him see himself all the way inside; that seeing himself with no expression, no features, no changing moods, was refreshing. Or will he only mention the way his hair was sticking up and out from all sides, the March wind at his back, waves whipped up into his face, no land in sight for miles? Moving towards her, recollecting her smile, her laugh before he'd excused himself, he reads her face all over again, takes back his seat and turns the woman's head; to correct his face in hers, to try out his new reflection, beginning from the moment he'd finished, zipped, tightened.

The White Ribbon

He heaves into her from behind, just before dinner. His arm has been damaged in an accident so afterwards she helps him with his zip. She then sees to herself. When they sit down, she talks about his time away, that one of his boy's didn't like her and that she was glad he was back. He looks at her and begins to hate what he sees. In the long eked-out silence, she knows she wasn't missed when he was in hospital, says so and he reflects the self-loathing right back at her. A strand of hair has come away from behind her ear and hangs down deliberately over the stew. One of his hands is in a sling, the other stays resolute near his pocket. She puts down her spoon, smiles and sniffs a laugh, then lays her head on the table like a plate, shifting it into position. She waits, one beat, two, three, then he takes his good hand from under the table, lowers it onto her hair, strokes the palm over her tied back locks, one beat, two. Later, after a few more dinners, he'll let her have what his bad hand can't say. She already knows. Next time the invisible line slung between the trees in his garden will kill him. Her head is resolute. The next scene is winter. Snow, closed wooden doors of a church and the remains of a crooked village.

The Lowering of Heads

In the tea-room of the library, when the sun is over the yard-arm, they wipe their mouths of the last swig of caffeine, return as to the field and work. In the reading-room, some plough through leaves and soil with a deft and respectful rustle, while others stifle a sigh, politely curse above the worms, and the smack of steel on stone. By night, long after the call for last requests, being here is like lying awake in an old dorm, in the minutes after the lights and sayings are put out. Some heads stay still and calm above the pillows, while others dream unquiet beneath the school's tight linen. They try and disguise the unrest, the fright behind their eyes. But watch closely; listen for the odd turn and flinch under white sheets that give the signs of war away and beware the birds that bomb the crops when the scarecrow looks behind him.

Play in the Rehearsal

As the table bolts to her left, glasses flail onto their backs and the ashtray skids like a puck through the whisky and ice. She flinches as a door smacks open, looks up to see 'Gentlemen' rock back into place. Picking up a Guinness coaster, she draws pools of swollen light into its corners and thinks of them by the sea, running from the waves, backs screaming to the shore. When he sits down his eyes resemble wet blue stones. The eye and the pint on the card-board square are pulp in the hand he has squashed; she twists out backwards to clean off the mess. 'Shall we try again?' His words meander in the air, unsure of how to land. I look out of the way of his eyes – the table is one move away from wasteland – any second now, she's going to jump.

Apple for Teeth

After nine years away, she looked her father in the face and froze. Covering her mouth with her hand she saw his fingers clenched round an apple, eaten to the core, red skin between his teeth, the flesh not quite ready for swallowing. 'It's alright dear, it's only apple,' he spluttered and after nine years she broke, not because they were together again, but because nobody had told her what to expect from a man last seen leaping on and off the furniture and hurled into a house with no windows, no door, no path, no address. So in the chaos of white falling loose inside his mouth, she saw apple for teeth, and broke because it was he who had told her otherwise and finally recognised how fear looked in his daughter's face.

Table Memoir

Pale and quiet in the face of such well-dressed wood, she waits to see what comes next; urges each minute on, less by speaking than watching and surveying the table change over the course of the evening. Progress is slow; she gets into the habit of looking down its grain and polished tide-lines, over the silver and glass, up the three-pronged candlestick, its crown of wicks in gold, dancing to the heat of the soup. When their heads are bowed, steam breaking at the family's skin, she watches them bless the food, while she prepares what she would say to the table. First a question: is the spoon in front of me for the soup, or the one at my elbow? And before you answer that, do I take the bread from the little plate to my left or right? And if I want some water from that jug sitting miles away, do I help myself or pour some for everyone and if everyone, how will I get up without scraping my chair, walk around all of them, lean in between each head without spilling a drop? And did you prefer life as a door? But the answers get rained on, the chatter so constant, so eloquent, so collected and excitedly thrown about its surface, that she gets stuck: can't hear, think nor speak. Today she remembers little of what was said, but recalls the hunger each night she cleared the table; mopping the telling puddles at her place and the crumbs that would give her away.

After Buñuel: *The Phantom of Liberty*

The girl is told it's rude to speak of hunger at the table. The other guests politely ignore her, continue smoking and reading their magazines. The conversation, in between articles, is about bodily waste and the growing rate of the population. The men calculate how much excrement would be evacuated, should birth continue in this way. The girl does not have much to offer, but restlessly scrawls on a piece of paper and shifts about on her potty. The adults sit on grown-up seats, all lids up, skirts hoisted hip-high, trousers ruffled by their ankles, satisfied on their porcelain, otherwise flushable if not for being placed round a table. Down the corridor to the left is a door that leads to the dining-room. It has a lock, a chair, a fold-away table attached to the wall and a food elevator, or dumb-waiter as the man who has excused himself, prefers to call it. He opens the door, turns the lock, surveys the cupboard-sized space, sits down, tucks the napkin into his shirt, pulls the table down to his knees and calls the lift. At the little door's opening, he reaches for the bottle of wine, glasses and a dish, based around poultry. At the first tear of the bird's leg, a knock on the door. *'C'est occupé!'* he cries, mouth filthy with food, his face turning indecent with the rest of the evening's episodic privacy.

The Gap in the Resolute Desk

A gift from Queen Victoria to Rutherford B. Hayes, the President's desk was built from rescued pieces of an arctic discovery vessel, H M S Resolute. Salvaged from the ocean's feast and made into several tables and desks to be scattered among Royals and Rulers, the wood's carvings, inscriptions and adjustments tell of its renewed tale all over the world. But at its heart, its centre, where there is nothing – a void, necessary for all desks – is the core of the piece; where the true stories are kept. During Roosevelt's reign, it was filled in by a hinged door, a modesty panel, requested by the leader to hide his leg braces. During Reagan's time, the desk was raised due to several close encounters between the wood and his knees. And during JFK's office, according to the words of his son, the panel became 'the secret door' and the covered gap, 'my house'. In the Oval Office, October 1963, JFK Jr. pokes his head out of the kneehole, while his father is reviewing papers above him, his mother is abroad and a photographer invited to take rare visual notes of Kennedy's family life. This private moment makes history three months later, after JFK is killed. One of the most revealed hiding places in America, the 'secret door' hosts the young boy's face peering out cautiously, while his father smiles contentedly above him. When the panel is shut, the Presidential seal shows – only one of four where the eagle faces left towards 13 arrows in his talon. In another shot, the boy is in his 'house', his face ever more wary of the camera's eye, while his father poses, thrusts out his arm and points a finger across the room from his chair. But from his wooden cave, his son can't see what his father can and focuses instead on the camera, on the camera-man and on us, the whole world, open-mouthed, hiding right in front of his eyes.

Derwent the Boy, Derwent the River

Coleridge's son, Derwent, very new to the full use of his faculties, in the summer of 1803 was on the brink of a fever. He spent the initial throws of his delirium running around the kitchen for so long 'that for the first time in his consciousness, he became giddy...turned pale with fright and repeatedly cried – 'The Kissen is walking away from Derwent' – pawing out his hands as if stopping it.' Part tipsy, part ecstatic, he tried to catch all the low-flying objects, grasping at wooden legs and cupboard doors. As the cabinets opened and closed, flew out from his hands that flexed with purpose at their wings, the stumpy supports of furniture tripped over themselves in puzzlement. Derwent was on a steep learning curve that week. Not days before, his father was explaining to his son the connection between sight and eyes. Derwent had never considered putting the two together, so Coleridge explained and then put the rest of his features to test. In helping his son work out what his tongue was for, his father asked him to hold it and try and say 'papa' – this he did 'and finding that he could not speak, he turned pale as death and in the reaction from fear flushed red and gave [him] a blow in the face.' Following this lesson, Derwent let his tongue and all his other features run free, while trying to pin wayward objects down. Coleridge watched carefully, took note, at his desk, by the river, and did all he could to follow.

Beam of Light

It doesn't appear to have a mouth, so how do you propose we feed it? The small boy makes his point, hands waving about his head. Today, there is no school and they have time to work this out. The boy sighs, brings his hands down towards his head and scratches; his friend moves his gaze purposefully between the boy and the table. The box in the kitchen has been speaking all morning, its wire grate radiating announcements, music, news, plays, weather, and nature. The words are formed inside, though how do they leave the box and land in the kitchen? They don't know what to call it, whether to hold it, dissect it, or make it listen. But they do decide it's hungry. On approach, however, the thing slips between stations and throws out the full charge of a river at storm: they scream, jump, hide under the table and creep out only when the enemy loses consciousness. One tiny hand emerges like a shy puppet, feels a button, turns it anti-clockwise and lands on the weather report. They learn of the sun outside the window, watch the way its light gives the thing a shadow, and hear the clouds that will smother it by the afternoon.

Of Kings and Men

The table slants under the weight of the television. At three o'clock there is a cartoon about a King who never smiles. It is someone else's job to make him laugh, for 'a sad King is a sad Kingdom.' Many kinds of men – jesters, jugglers, dancers, clowns, musicians – try to lift his corners, but their jokes, fiddles, exploding colours, bold and foolish moves, fail to touch him. One by one they are asked to leave, scratching their heads and dragging their instruments back through the gates. One day, the King is presented with a last hope. When the Crown looks up, he is far from impressed. Before him, an ordinary looking man, unshaven, with an unsure bow and on straightening, almost nothing in him that looks at all upright. But two things about the man strike his Majesty: he carries in his hand a long white feather and in his eye, a focus so hungry, so intent, that the King – for the first time in his recent reign – sits up, wakes up and gives him his undivided attention. The man moves towards him, stands so close the King can feel his breath. He freezes, the room freezes: the Court, the Throne, Crown, Windows, Clock and Land hold their breath. The King wants to push the man away, rises higher into his chair, opens his mouth as if to scream, but instead begins to laugh and laughs again until his Crown falls to the ground and he follows in its wake, holding himself in shame when he is on the floor, his garments loose around him. There is no harm done other than this: he has been tickled, that is all, tickled by a man with a long white feather. But, the girl watching, doesn't see this, nor get this and grows fixated on a broken King: remembers only a scream that was never sounded, clothes that were lifted without permission and the eyes of the King as he looked around for his next move, seconds before his face cracked open and poured all of his sadness away.

Invisible People

We meet them in the switches of lights and kettles; hear them in the language of cartoons: *click, whirr, whoosh, BOOM! bubble, fizz, kerplunk*. When we leave the couch at a Soap break and reach for cups, they raise their levels and make our tea like ghosts. They do not spy through windows, but know us by patterns; we give them our habits on a plate and they feed them. Read most easily in leaves, matches and Soaps, when sport and drama peak in league and story, they are behind every goal and cliff hanger. And when our hands rush up to our faces, they hum over the cries, fill the pitch, pub and kitchen with surges of light and follow us around the room as we win and lose all over the place.

The Author's Tour

The voice sits down in front of them. Its story at first floats like a cloud over their faces and as it lightly skims their eyes, he pictures himself as an old oak tree at the head of a field, a small herd of cows beginning to wake, gather upwards and tug on the morning's grass. The voice begins to unpack the tale, treading amidst the comfortable familiarity of its work and their heads slowly begin to fill. Songs are sung in buses winding up ancient hills. Men play chess outside their houses, their hands adept at moving pawns, queens and knights. Washing hangs above them high in the alleyways, zigzagging from balcony to balcony, shutter to shutter. Money is passed in old thousands across café tables that trim the Squares. The notes disappear in coffee and the slick weave of waiters. Violins and accordions dance near hats and cups and markets bloom in fruit and awnings. Birds peck, twitch, then suddenly storm upwards, hurling the ground towards the sky. There is a fight, a shot from above, a tower maybe, bells harangue the place, a white shirt bleeds through a hole. The voice draws to a close. His tongue is tired. The faces are chewing on the sentences and their eyes are narrowing towards the next stage; nothing between him and them but a rickety table, balancing pen, books, glass and his knotted hand scrabbling around for something to say.

The Book Launch

An old man tilts his head towards the woman beside him. He doesn't want to tell her anything, but she hears what he might have said. Their shoes touch and a flinch shoots into her shoulder. The host gets up from the table, fingers the painted book spines, tugs on one twice his own height and width, shouts out the title and author, grunts comically under the weight as he introduces the next reader. Gales, uproars of laughter animate the audience; their heads roll, slide and jump about like objects on a waking fault-line. The woman is freezing, despite the huddle of chairs and the warmth of the listeners; shudders again at the possibility of him leaning in, crossing her foot, touching the back of her head. She witnesses lines everywhere – in the panels, the windows, the table on the stage, the painted books and shelves behind the speakers, the leading of the glass saints. Vertical, horizontal, the whole place is cut up. She feels them moving awkwardly inside the structure; the setting puts their old grace to shame. Speech darts in and out of the margins from the stage; sometimes etiquette keeps their tone in company with the setting, sometimes it encourages them to take risks. Mostly though, what she hears and what they take away are their tempered conversations coming in through glass. Filtering through the reds, whites and blues accompanied by carefully snatched looks that step over the papered cracks accordingly. Appropriately. They are, have become a safely closing paragraph. A sentence that leaves things at that and gives them no reason to go back inside again.

At R. S. Thomas's Table

At the College, there were two tables, one for the English, one for the Welsh. Traditionally you ate at the table of your language, but he sat at both. Spending more time seated with the English, when among the Welsh, he was laughed at once for the way he pronounced spoon, *llwy*. The surface landscape of cutlery, glass, condiments, napkins and chairs all seemed much the same until they were spoken, but any young man who attempted to cross the bridge, became a sharp glint in one eye and a blank reflection in the other. Once a term there was a day when the men were silent. The languages unspoken, they met, went for walks and planned a day of wordless fun. Thoughts loved and warred equally; shifted or spilled out through gestures and looks and when the day was over, they returned to their seats, their bodies careful to remember, one was for the English and one for the Welsh.

The Wait

Black chairs around black tables, splashed with a white net cloth. Music in the kitchen, a cigarette and wine break after the cakes have been cut and the tea poured. A couple take the table by the window and realise all too late that their view of the street is hidden from them by a thin wet curtain of steam. They wipe peep-holes on the glass when the conversation allows; stare onto shutting shops, comment on the quaintness of the apologetic phrasing: 'We will be back tomorrow!' 'Gone for a much-needed break.' The woman looks down, drawls her sleeve over the table's previous guest. The man's eye follows the crumbs to the floor; an observation that may come up later or tomorrow, but he leaves it for now. Yawning, he tips back in his chair, lets his gaze stretch the length of the corridor to the kitchen. The woman in the back is still on her break, wondering between drags who else has slipped in and whether she has the energy to emerge onto the floor and be appreciated, cake by home-made cake. When he sets himself upright, she turns, hears the feet of chair legs graze the wood, scrunches her filter onto a plate and makes a bee-line for him, trying hard not to bite her tongue.

The Shared Surface

The table holds a book, two twinned elbows, one knuckle, and a palm, flat, save the scrape of a nail, as one man's finger rises into a hunch. Each time he reads aloud, his familiar knocks a closed hand hard on the wood. This is stop, a comma, a semi-colon, a rest. When the knuckle blows the surface again he goes on. The man's mouth repeats the last line; his voice treads the words in the dark, listening for the slate thin over a mineshaft. Gets as far as the next sentence and knock, stops his breath and waits. The rhythm is far from predictable, the place in the writing no indicator, no warning. A whole paragraph passes, is cut at the word, 'tell.' The reader raises his eyes towards his. He looks back at him, lowers the lids, covers his face with one hand, comes down, bone on oak with the other. 'There is nothing left to tell.' He goes on, his voice rivered, pebbles shifting up from the bed. Crack. This time he starts, glowers towards the covert face, a shine insisting above his mouth, a slight heat across his frown. Cloud gathers in the room; their long white hair closing in on the day. The knots in the wood, peacock eyes, black stares; the years, the rings, his creasing forehead, sand after the tide has pulled out. Reading on, the table waits. Another bit pummelled in, another bit taken out; one man's splinter, another man's bruise.

The Chipping Forecast

The man with eyes buried deep into his face pulls on black rubber gloves. He looks across at his guest and asks if it would help to talk about pain and coping with it. The man with eyes bulging far from his face has parted with his money again, this time to be injected with a chip. A pip removed from the apple and put back into the flesh; a miniature edition of the world inside him that can be read from outside, by anyone, anywhere. When he starts, 'Mr?' he is asked to call him 'Simon'. 'Simon, does it work underwater?' The answer is 'as far as we know' and the man, also called Simon, is happy with this. Flattening his hand on the table, the man with the needle pinches the space between his thumb and neighbouring finger and praises it for its cushioning. Simon says the pain talk might be helpful actually. The chip is bobbing about in alcohol, fished out and dropped into the syringe's end. There is a tag intended for pets that came with the injection kit, but it is swiftly removed. Simon swabs Simon's hand with iodine, carefully prods and pulls up a fold of skin to peak the flesh. With the other hand he directs the syringe just below the skin's surface, drives the needle's handle down, and the chip disappears. Simon's face is dry. Simon's face is wet. A small crowd applauds. The first subject of the day has been successfully planted.

Square of Light: The Artist is Present I

A table in an atrium; a square of light. Two chairs at the table face each other, the artist in one, the other empty, an open invitation. Anyone, from anywhere, can sit with her, for as long or as little as they like. Over the course of three months, the artist looks into more than a thousand pairs of eyes. Halfway through the performance she takes the table away. Without a plane on which to lean, or slump or rest, the viewers become the viewees. Some of them cry. Not only are their faces exposed, but their legs or the absence of them. They become a body, not just a section of one and if they have ghosts for limbs, they become a story of that body. They don't tell her and she doesn't ask. There is no table anymore, no speaking, no leaning on elbows, no hidden shifting of shoes, just looking. Lives leak, itch, burn, smile, wince, blink, twitch, close, open, sleep, wake, stutter through their eyes. She catches and collects every drop; becomes a diary of what they don't say.

The Artist is Present II

Upon a table, she places 72 objects, some of which could give pleasure and others pain. The audience members are allowed to choose any thing and use it on her in any way they desire, while the artist sits by the table for six hours and waits to see what her changing company will do with a rose, treacle, knife, fork, salt, a gun, vase of water, feather, a glass frame... Tentative at first, not knowing if it is safe to touch or approach her with their weapon of choice, the audience grow bolder as the hours goes by. A stroke of a feather over her hair, a dab of water on her skin, change and move edgeways halfway through the performance. Drenched with the remaining water as it tips onto her neck, down her breasts, stomach, knees and feet, the rose adds blood to the mix as its thorns dot her stomach. When one person points the gun at her head, another takes it away. When another cuts into her clothes, another pours treacle over her damp head. She is mocked with a fan, quick, slow, quick wind around her body, then crowned with a plastic tiara and forced to smoke the feather. A sitting Jesus. A present King George. A quiet place, pillaged. A stream ending in a storm-fuelled sea, a field, gutted and built-over, an artist inviting us to look at her, then ourselves in quick, slow, quick succession.

Jane Monson has an MA in Creative Writing from the University of East Anglia, and a Ph.D in Creative and Critical Writing from Cardiff University. Based in Cambridge, she is a book-seller for Cambridge University Press and a freelance writer and teacher. Jane has been short-listed for an Eric Gregory award and commended by Poetry London and the New Writing Partnership. She has reviewed poetry collections for *Magma*, and the *British Journal of Canadian Studies*. Her poetry is widely anthologised and published in magazines. Her first collection of prose poetry was *Speaking Without Tongues*, (Cinnamon Press) followed by *This Line Is Not For Turning* (Cinnamon Press), a critically acclaimed anthology of contemporary British prose poetry, which she edited.